TEN THOUSAND POISONOUS PLANTS IN THE WORLD

PAUL ROCKETT

W
FRANKLIN WATTS
LONDON • SYDNEY

Franklin Watts
This edition published in 2016 by
The Watts Publishing Group

Editor: Rachel Cooke
Design and illustration: Mark Ruffle
www.rufflebrothers.com

Dewey number: 581.6'59
ISBN: 978 1 4451 4743 7

Printed in China

Franklin Watts
An imprint of
Hachette Children's Group
Part of The Watts Publishing Group
Carmelite House
50 Victoria Embankment
London EC4Y 0DZ

An Hachette UK company.
www.hachette.co.uk

www.franklinwatts.co.uk

MIX
Paper from
responsible sources
FSC® C104740
FSC
www.fsc.org

Picture credits: AVTG/istockphoto: 21c; Peter
Barritt/Alamy: 23br; Charles Brutlag/Shutterstock:
15tc; Chevanon/Shutterstock: 21t; Ethan Daniels/
Shutterstock: 23bl; digital94086/istockphoto: 29b;
Dimijana/Shutterstock: 10c; Edith Dorsey Raff/
Alamy: 11t; Dr John Dransfield/RBG Kew: 9b;
EcoPrint/Shutterstock: 23cr; Mark Goddard/
istockphoto: 11b; Volodymyr Goinyk/Shutterstock: 22b;
Chris Hill/Shutterstock: 15tr; Ioflo69/istockphoto: 29c;
Juniors Bildarchiv Gmbh/Alamy: 23tr; kanusommer/
Shutterstock: 29t; Tamara Kulikova/Shutterstock:
24b. Majeczka/Shutterstock: front cover bc. Andrew
McRobb/RBG Kew: 9t; Mexrix/Shutterstock:front cover
tr; Jeng Niamwhan/Shutterstock: 15tl; Dr Moreley
Read/Shutterstock: 4b, 23cl; Peter Ryan: 9ca; Sanevich/
Shutterstock: 28; Sursad/Shutterstock: 25t; Saru T/
Shutterstock: 9c. Jordan Tan/Shutterstock: front cover
c; Timobaggibs/Shutterstock: 17t; Natalie Spelier
Ufermann/Shutterstock: 20c; Zhuda/Shutterstock: 27t.

*Throughout the book you are given data relating
to various pieces of information covering the topic.
The numbers will most likely be an estimation based
on research made over a period of time and in a
particular area. Some other research may reach
a different set of data, and all these figures may
change with time as new research and information is
gathered. The numbers provided within this book are
believed to be correct at the time of printing and have
been sourced from the following sites:*
algaeindustrymagazine.com; antarctica.ac.uk;
aquaphoenix.com; bbc.co.uk; bbka.org.uk;
belladonnakillz.com; bio.umass.edu; biologie.uni-
hamburg.de; botany.org; britannica.com; caes.uga.edu;
chemistry.about.com; conifersaroundtheworld.com;
conservatree.org; cultivatorscorner.com; currentresults.
com; cuyabenolodge.com; desertusa.com; dhs.
wisconsin.gov; education.nationalgeographic.co.uk;
encyclopedia2.thefreedictionary.com; eoearth.org;
equalexchange.coop; fairtrade.org.uk; gardenorganic.
org.uk; goarticles.com; guinnessworldrecords.com;
imnh.isu.edu; iucn.org; iucnredlist.org; kew.org;
kids.britannica.com; livingrainforest.org; metoffice.
gov.uk; microscopy-uk.org.uk; naturalfibres2009.
org; nature.com; news.discovery.com; news.
nationalgeographic.co.uk; nhm.ac.uk; oxtreegen.
com; princeton.edu; rainforestconcern.org; rfs.org.
uk; sciencedaily.com; scienceforkids.kidipede.com;
statisticbrain.com; svalbardflora.net; telegraph.
co.uk; topnotchtreeservicestjoemo.com; thompson-
morgan.com; tropicaltraditions.com; vcbio.science.
ru.nl; woodlands.co.uk; woodlandtrust.org.uk;
worldanimalfoundation.net.

CONTENTS

Plants can be found all over the world.

They are living organisms that, unlike animals, cannot move by themselves.

PLANTS WERE THE FIRST LIVING ORGANISMS ON EARTH

More than **2,000,000,000 years ago**, a form of algae started life underwater. Around **473,000,000 years ago** liverworts started growing on land. These evolved into many different plant forms. The last form, flowering plants, appeared **140,000,000 years ago**.

Plants produce their own food. They absorb energy from the Sun, which along with carbon dioxide and water, enables them to make food and oxygen. This process is called photosynthesis.

**Conifers
290,000,000
years ago**

**Flowering
plants
140,000,000
years ago**

**Algae
2,000,000,000
years ago**

**Ferns
360,000,000
years ago**

**Mosses
470,000,000
years ago**

**Liverworts
473,000,000
years ago**

Plants provide the world with oxygen, which is key to the survival of all animals. From plants, we also get food, wood and medicines.

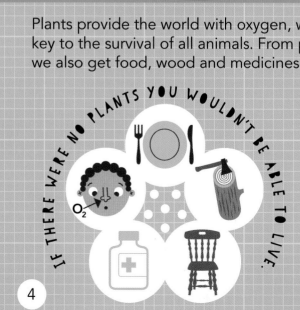

IF THERE WERE NO PLANTS YOU WOULDN'T BE ABLE TO LIVE.

O₂

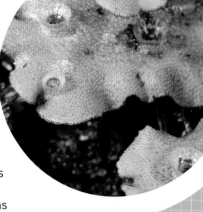

Liverworts are often put into the same plant group as mosses. However there are differences, such as their leaf and root structures are not as clearly defined as those of mosses.

BOTANY

Botany is the scientific study of plants. A botanist is a plant explorer, who studies plant structures and how they grow. They may do this in a science lab, or outside in the plant's environment, such as the rainforest or garden.

Numbers play an important role in botany. They are used for calculating statistics and looking for patterns within cell structures and rates of growth.

COUNTING THE RINGS OF A TREE

You can work out the age of a fallen tree by counting the rings on its stump. Each ring represents one year of growth. A large distance between each ring tells us that it was a wet and rainy year. A small distance between the rings tells us it was a dry year.

This tree was 14 years old.
- First year growth
- Rainy year
- Dry year
- Scar from forest fire
- 14th year of growth
- Bark

COUNTING PLANTS WITHIN A FIELD

If you wanted to get an estimate of the kind of plant life and the amount of plant life that grows in a nearby field, get hold of a metre square and throw it into the field. Wherever it lands, count and record the plants that you find.

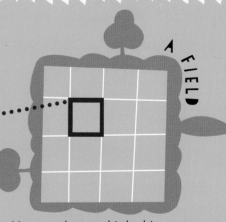

A metre square is a good size – it shouldn't take too long to count all of the life that you capture within it.

You can then multiply this amount by the size of the field. This will give you an estimate of the number of plants and plant species within the entire field.

Plants grow all around us, in gardens and parks, but also in less accessible places, such as rainforests, deserts and at the bottom of the ocean.

The large number of plant species all over the world makes the task of counting and identifying each one impossible. However, many people attempt to do this, with differing results. The number of plant species identified varies from **300,000** to **380,000**.

The World Conservation Unit estimates the number of plant species as being **321,212**. They have divided plant life into **five categories**: flowering, conifers, ferns, mosses and liverworts, and red and green algae.

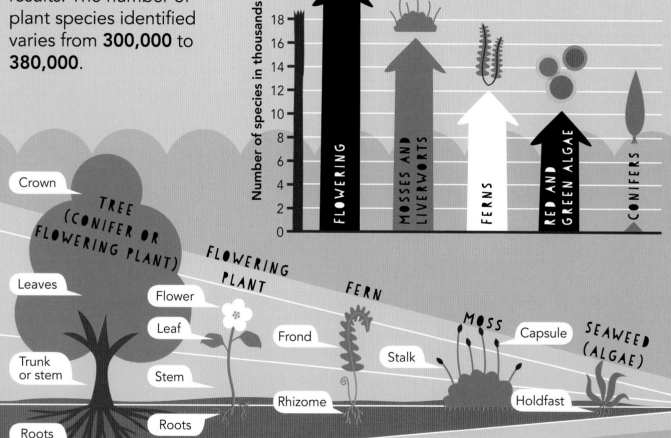

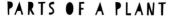

PARTS OF A PLANT
Most plants have roots, leaves and stems. Plants may have parts that differ from each other, but they all have elements that help them perform similar functions. For example, the frond of the fern is similar to the leaf of a tree, the capsule on moss is similar to a flower.

ROOTS

Roots keep plants firmly connected to the ground. In flowering and coniferous plants there are two main kinds of roots:

Fibrous roots • • • • • • • • •
These are spread out in many directions and all tend to be the same size.

• **Tap roots**
This is one large root with smaller roots coming off it. Root vegetables, such as carrots and parsnips, are tap roots.

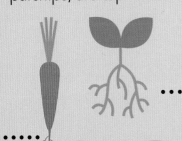

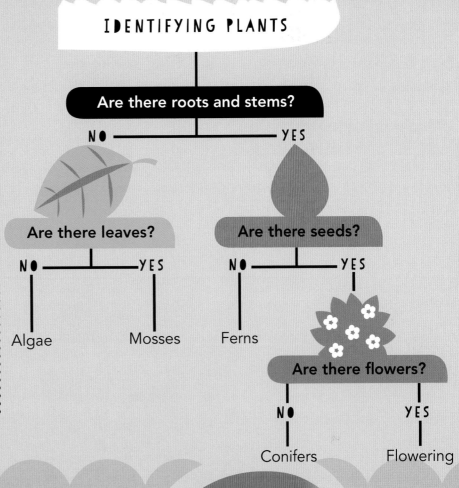

Are there roots and stems?

NO ——————————— YES

Are there leaves?

NO ————— YES

Algae   Mosses

Are there seeds?

NO ————— YES

Ferns

Are there flowers?

NO   YES

Conifers   Flowering

ALGAE

Not all scientists include algae as a type of plant. Algae do not always appear with a root-like structure, with some, like the microscopic diatom, existing as just a single, individual cell.

DIATOM

Algae are largely found in areas of water, on the surface or bottom of lakes, rivers and oceans. Some types of seaweed and kelp are forms of algae. Many scientists believe that the blue-green algae were the first living things to appear on planet Earth.

SEAWEED

FUNGI

Fungi are organisms that includes mushrooms, yeasts and moulds. They used to be part of the plant kingdom, but since 1969 they have been separated into their own kingdom. They may look like plants, but they have a different cell structure and don't produce their own food. In fact, many scientists believe that fungi are more closely related to animals than to plants.

7

64,242 PLANTS ESTIMATED AT RISK OF EXTINCTION

Some scientists have estimated that one in five species of plant is at risk of dying out. If there are 321,212 species of plant, that's 64,242 plants at risk.

THREATS TO PLANT LIFE

The main threat to plant life is caused by humans, largely through the clearance of natural habitats for agriculture and industrial development.

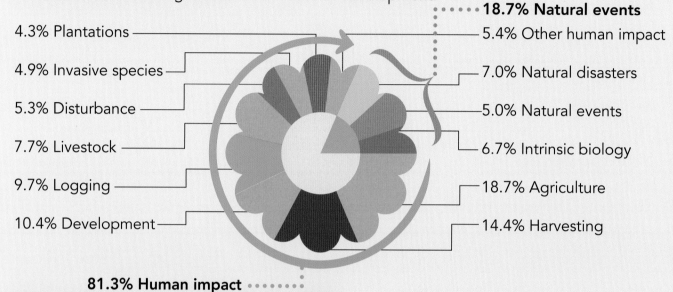

4.3% Plantations

4.9% Invasive species

5.3% Disturbance

7.7% Livestock

9.7% Logging

10.4% Development

18.7% Natural events

5.4% Other human impact

7.0% Natural disasters

5.0% Natural events

6.7% Intrinsic biology

18.7% Agriculture

14.4% Harvesting

81.3% Human impact

FROM VULNERABLE TO EXTINCT

The large number of plant species makes it very difficult for botanists to assess the actual number that are at risk of extinction. The International Union for the Conservation of Nature took a sample of **15,674 plant species** and found that **121** were extinct and **9,390** were at threat of extinction.

The plants were placed in the following categories:

Vulnerable: high risk of endangerment in the wild

Endangered: high risk of extinction in the wild

Critically endangered: extremely high risk of extinction in the wild

Extinct in the wild: known only to survive in botanic gardens

Extinct: no known individuals remaining

Out of the **15,674 plants** assessed, just under **60%** were found to fall into the vulnerable to extinct categories. If we apply this percentage to the **321,212 species of plants** then it's possible that **192,432 plants** are at risk. That's about **three in five plant species** at risk!

RESULTS FROM SAMPLE SELECTION:

15,674 PLANT SPECIES

Vulnerable: 4,914

Endangered: 2,655

Critically endangered: 1,821

Extinct: 121

VULNERABLE

Name: Eastern Cape giant cycad
Plant category: cycad, a species that links ferns and conifers
Habitat: coastal areas, riverbanks and mountain foothills of South Africa
Threats: destruction for holiday resort developments and use in traditional medicines.
Population number: estimated at **10,000** Thought to have declined by **30%** in the past **50 years**

ENDANGERED

Name: Bentgrass
Plant category: flowering
Habitat: rocky slopes and open patches of land on islands off the South Atlantic Ocean
Threat: erosion of land and fires; introduction of alien plants in habitats preventing their growth
Population number: estimated that fewer than **250** exist in the wild

CRITICALLY ENDANGERED

Name: Amazon lily
Plant category: flowering
Habitat: Colombian rainforests
Threat: large-scale deforestation
Population number: unknown. Not been recorded in the wild since 1853. Thought to be extinct

CRITICALLY ENDANGERED

Name: Jellyfish tree
Plant category: flowering
Habitat: granite slopes near the coast of islands in the Indian Ocean
Population number: thought to be extinct in 1930 until six trees were found in 1970. Today, **50 trees** are known to exist.

EXTINCT

Name: Cry pansy
Plant category: flowering
History: originally from France, growing in areas around limestone, its habitat was largely destroyed through quarrying. Plant population also drastically reduced as it became a popular flower for collectors. Last seen in 1927.

MOST THREATENED

Amphibians

Coral

The world's plants are as threatened with extinction as mammals.

Plants and Mammals

Birds

LEAST THREATENED

LIFE FORMS AT THREAT OF EXTINCTION

THERE ARE TEN THOUSAND POISONOUS PLANTS IN THE WORLD

Plants are unable to run and hide from their predators and so have developed other means of protecting themselves. Some plants, like rose bushes or cacti, have thorns or spines to discourage animals from coming near them. Other plants have poison, which can make an animal incredibly sick or even kill them.

There are around **10,000 poisonous plant species**. Their poison is released by touching or eating them; some cause short-term illness, others death.

Poisonous plants have toxins that can be found in their sap, leaves or berries.

MOST POISONOUS

Many botanists consider the castor oil plant to be the most poisonous plant in the world. The castor oil plant grows in tropical conditions and produces a highly toxic seed, called the castor bean.

CASTOR BEANS

THE BELLADONNA PLANT can be found growing wild in Europe, North America and South-west Asia. Also known as deadly nightshade, all parts of this plant are poisonous.

If you eat a castor bean that breaks open inside your digestive system, you may find that within:

2-3 HOURS — you experience a burning sensation in your mouth and throat, stomach pain and diarrhoea containing traces of blood;

1-3 DAYS — you experience severe dehydration and a decrease in urine;

3-5 DAYS — you die.

Eating a single leaf will kill you.

Eating **five berries** will kill you.

Eating the roots will kill you.

STINGING PLANTS

STINGING NETTLES

The most common stinging plant found in Europe, North America and parts of Asia is the stinging nettle.

Nettles have hairy leaves, and hairs on their stem.

Each hair has a bulbous tip. Upon contact this tip breaks off to leave a sharp, needle-like tube that pierces the skin, injecting a toxin. This toxin can leave raised bumps on the skin and an itching sensation that can last up to **12 hours**.

GYMPIE-GYMPIE STINGING TREE

The gympie-gympie stinging tree, found in the rainforests of Australia and Indonesia, is the only stinging plant that is believed to cause death from its stings. It has been known to kill dogs and horses that have brushed up against it.

A gympie sting has been described as like being burnt with hot acid and electrocuted at the same time!

CARNIVOROUS PLANTS

All plants get their food through photosynthesis. However some plants are themselves predators and will trap and eat animals in order to get more nutrients to help them grow.

PITCHER PLANTS

There are **120 species** of pitcher plant. The giant pitcher plant is the largest of all carnivorous plants. Discovered in the Philippines, it produces a sweet-smelling nectar inside its jar-like head.

Nectar attracts insects and small mammals that fall inside.

Creatures are unable to climb out due to the sticky walls inside and end up dissolving in a pool of acid and enzymes.

VENUS FLYTRAPS

The Venus flytrap eats small insects, enclosing them within its traps.

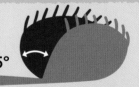

The trap opens at an average of **45 degrees**. 45°

The trap closes when an insect touches a single hair twice, or **two separate hairs** within **20 seconds** of each other.

OXYGEN IS RENEWED BY PLANTS EVERY TWO THOUSAND YEARS

The food we eat and the oxygen we breathe are both formed by plants through a process called photosynthesis.

PHOTOSYNTHESIS INGREDIENTS

LIGHT ENERGY + WATER H_2O + CARBON DIOXIDE O C O + CHLOROPHYLL

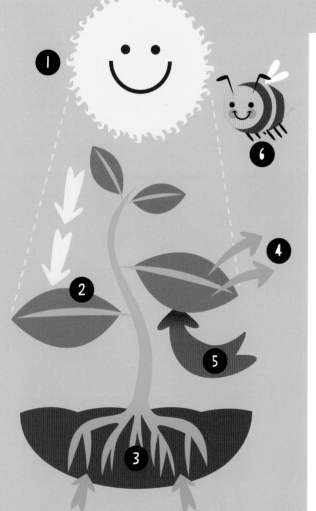

STEP 1
Light from the Sun shines down onto a plant. The plant's cells absorb this light.

STEP 2
Inside the plant cells is a substance called chlorophyll. Chlorophyll traps the Sun's light.

STEP 3
Water is absorbed into the plant through its roots underground. Water is made up of the elements hydrogen and oxygen.

STEP 4
Inside the plant, the oxygen and hydrogen from the water separate from each other; the oxygen is released into the atmosphere.

STEP 5
Carbon dioxide from the air is absorbed through the plant's leaves. The carbon dioxide combines with the hydrogen to make a form of sugar the plant can use as food.

STEP 6
Animals also use the sugar produced by the plants as food.

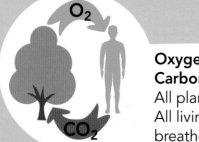

Oxygen = O_2
Carbon dioxide = CO_2
All plants release oxygen into the Earth's atmosphere.
All living creatures breathe in oxygen to keep them alive and breathe out carbon dioxide, which is absorbed by plants.

FOOD CHAINS

Plants are at the start of every food chain. All animal life depends upon plants for food.

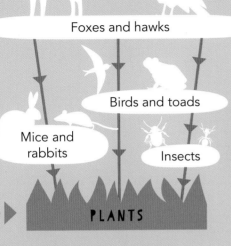

Foxes and hawks

Birds and toads

Mice and rabbits

Insects

PLANTS

CHLOROPHYLL COLOUR

Chlorophyll is the reason why most plants are green. During photosynthesis plants absorb the different colours that make up the Sun's light. However chlorophyll is not able to absorb the colour green and so it reflects it back, which is why we see green plants.

REFLECTED GREEN

LEAF

THE EARTH'S OXYGEN

Scientists believe that when the Earth was formed **4,500,000,000 years ago**, its atmosphere was largely made up of carbon dioxide. The process of photosynthesis by plants meant that the proportion of oxygen increased. This increase in oxygen helped develop the variety of life that is now on Earth.

OXYGEN

70% comes from algae and small organisms in the oceans ·········

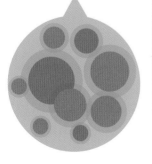

28% comes from tropical rainforests ·········

2% other ·········

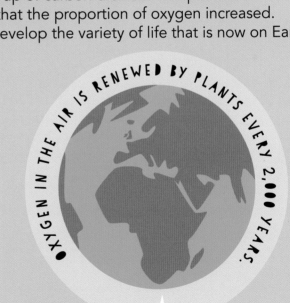

OXYGEN IN THE AIR IS RENEWED BY PLANTS EVERY 2,000 YEARS.

Each carbon dioxide molecule in the atmosphere is absorbed into a plant every **200 years**.

A POMEGRANATE CAN HAVE AS MANY AS 1,370 SEEDS

Flowering plants and conifers grow from seeds and create seeds.

Conifers have their seeds protected inside cones. A cone's scales open up to release its seeds.

Flowering plants have their seeds hidden within their fruit, although some plants, like corn and other grains, have their fruit and seeds fused together.

One apple can produce as many as **20 seeds**.

A pomegranate can contain as many as **1,370 seeds**.

Some orchids have seed pods that can hold around **3,000,000,000 seeds**.

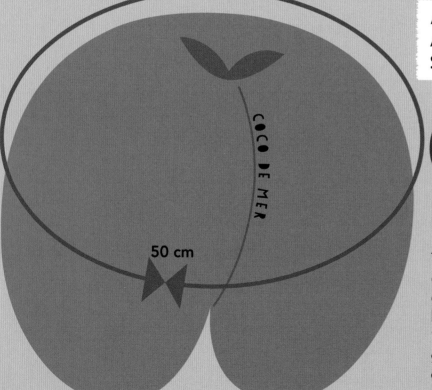

COCO DE MER

50 cm

A NUT IS A FRUIT MADE OF A HARD SHELL AND A SEED INSIDE.

Shell

HAZELNUT

Kernel

The largest seed in the world comes from a nut from a plant called coco de mer. The hard shell has two lobes giving it the name 'the double coconut'. It can have a girth measuring up to **50 cm**, and can weigh up to **17.6 kg**.

SEED DISPERSAL

Plants disperse their seeds in different ways, so that when plants grow they don't crowd each other or have to compete for water or light.

WATER
Plants on a riverbank or seashore drop their seeds into the water, which then float away to grow further away. Some coconuts have floated **2,000 km** before finding dry land.

EXPLOSIONS
Some plants have seed pods that explode, scattering their seeds. As a pod begins to dry out it shrinks. At the same time the seeds ripen and grow bigger, and burst out of the pod.

ANIMAL
Some plants have seeds that are sticky or have small hooks that attach to animal fur. The animal then transports the seeds to a new place. Animals and birds also poo out the seeds that are in the fruit they eat.

WIND
Some fruits are so light that they and their seeds can be blown away by the wind. The seeds of the dandelion flower get dispersed by the wind.

The dandelion flower has bright yellow florets. When these florets die out, seeds grow on the flower head.

SPORES
Mosses and ferns are non-seed plants. They produce spores. Spores are tiny reproductive cells. On ferns, they are often contained within tiny brown-black dots on the leaf. On mosses they can be found in their capsules. The spores are transported from the plants by wind or water. A single fern frond can hold up to **750,000 spores**.

One dandelion flower head produces **200 seeds**.

TRAVELLING DISTANCE:

99.5 per cent of dandelion seeds travel less than **10 metres**

0.05 per cent travel more than **10 metres**

One kilometre

0.014 per cent travel more than **one kilometre**

IT CAN TAKE 3½ WEEKS FROM SEED TO APPLE

When a seed starts to grow it begins a process called germination. This starts with a tiny root and shoot sprouting out through the coating of the seed.

PARTS OF A SEED

········Shoot
········Seed coat
········Food store
········Root

Leaves

Plant

Seedling

Stem

GERMINATION

Seed

WHEN DO SEEDS GROW?

Seeds can survive for a long time before they begin to grow into a plant. The time it takes for a seed to germinate depends on it receiving enough water and being in the right type of soil at the correct temperature.

Number of days for a seed to germinate according to temperature

Degrees C °	0°	5°	10°	15°	20°	25°	30°	36°
Parsnip	172	57	27	20	14	15	32	
Onion	136	50	13	7	5	4	4	13
Carrot		50	17	10	7	7	6	9
Pea		46	14	9	8	8	6	9
Tomato			43	14	14	6	6	9
Pepper			25	25	13	8	8	9
Watermelon			12		12	12	4	3

CAMPION

The oldest seed to grow into a plant was dated as **32,000 years old**. It grew into a narrow-leafed campion, a flowering plant native to Siberia. It's believed to have been buried by a squirrel during the Ice Age.

RATES OF GROWTH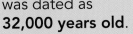

Once germinated, it can take an apple seed **six to ten years** to grow into a tree and bear fruit. However, it's very hard to grow an apple tree that will produce a large crop from seeds. Because of this, fruit-bearing apple trees are mainly grown from grafting, which can help them produce fruit more quickly. Grafting is a technique whereby parts of two plants are joined together. To achieve this, the stem of one plant's rootstock needs to be cut and joined to the stem of another plant.

Grafting

Rootstock

Rootstock can determine the plant's eventual size. Apple tree rootstock is sold with a tag telling the buyer how big their tree, once grafted, will grow.

THE SIZES ARE:

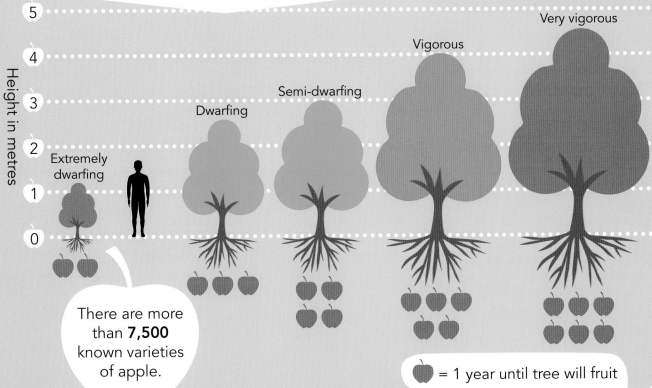

Height in metres

5
4
3
2
1
0

Very vigorous

Vigorous

Semi-dwarfing

Dwarfing

Extremely dwarfing

There are more than **7,500** known varieties of apple.

 = 1 year until tree will fruit

THERE ARE MORE THAN 300 TYPES OF HONEY

Honey is made from nectar that bees collect from flowers. While collecting nectar, bees also collect pollen, taking part in the process of plant pollination.

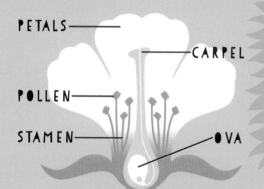

PETALS

CARPEL

POLLEN

STAMEN

OVA

Before flowers can produce fruit and seeds, they must be pollinated. This happens when the pollen from a flower joins to an ova hidden inside a flower.

Flowers contain stamens, at the top of which is the pollen. Flowers also have a carpel which holds an ova that the pollen needs to reach in order to allow the plant to grow its seeds and fruit.

POLLINATORS
Pollination is enabled by pollinators. They take the pollen from one flower to another. Pollinators include the wind, waves, human activity and animals such as:

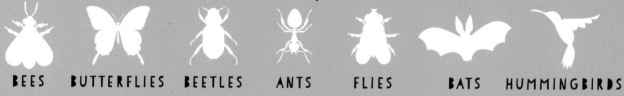

BEES   BUTTERFLIES   BEETLES   ANTS   FLIES   BATS   HUMMINGBIRDS

An estimated one out of every three bites of food comes to us through the work of animal pollinators.

ANIMAL POLLINATION
Many insects and birds feed off flowers. They are attracted to them by their bright colours and sweet smells.

Pollen is sticky and attaches itself to the creatures that have been drawn to the flower.

When the creature then visits another of these flowers, the pollen gets rubbed from its body onto the top of the carpel.

Once the pollen has attached itself to the carpel, it travels down to join the ova. The plant has now been pollinated as the pollen and ova join together to make seeds.

Some flowers are pollinated by the wind. Their pollen is carried through the air.

HAY FEVER

Pollen contains proteins that can cause an allergic reaction in some people. This is known as hay fever.

Symptoms:

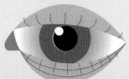
RUNNY NOSE

SNEEZING

ITCHY EYES

FLOWER POLLEN

Causes:

TREE POLLEN

GRASS POLLEN

BEES

It takes a colony of around **74,132 bees** to pollinate one hectare of fruit trees.

ONE HECTARE

A worker bee produces **1/10 teaspoon of honey** in its lifetime.

While collecting the pollen, bees feed off the nectar from flowers, which they carry back to their hives to make honey.

There are more than **300 different types of honey**, each type made from the nectar of a different flower.

THE TALLEST TREE IS 115.54 METRES HIGH

Trees are the tallest free-standing living things in the world. They also live longer than any other organism on Earth.

The oldest tree is a jurupa oak tree, in California, USA. It is said to be **13,000 years old**, making it the oldest living organism.
The oldest person to have lived reached the age of **122 years old**.
If the life of the oldest tree were measured as being **24 hours**, then the oldest person would have been alive for **14 minutes and 30 seconds** of that time.

12 hours   12 hours

14 minutes and 30 seconds

Lifespan of oldest person

Lifespan of oldest tree

The tree with the broadest trunk is a Montezuma cypress, in Oaxaca, Mexico. The trunk's diameter is **14 metres**, with a girth of **42 metres**.

The tallest living tree is a coast redwood, growing in the Redwood National Park, California, USA. It measures **115.54 metres** high.

The smallest tree is the dwarf willow tree. It rarely grows above **five centimetres**.

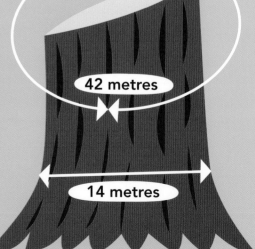

42 metres

14 metres

Tallest man to have lived: **2.72 metres**

TREE, SHRUB OR HERBACEOUS PLANT?

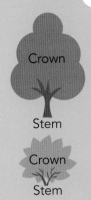

Crown

Stem

Crown

Stem

The difference between trees and shrubs is in the growth form of the stem. Trees have a single woody stem from which branches grow to form a crown. Shrubs have multiple woody stems that arise at ground level forming a crown at a lower level.

A herbaceous plant is a plant that does not have much wood and its stems are green and soft. You may hear people say that bananas grow on banana trees, but the banana actually grows on a herbaceous plant known as musa.

DECIDUOUS TREES

Deciduous plants are those that lose all of their leaves for part of the year. Depending on the region, this usually coincides with winter, or the dry season. The leafless trees need less water. Before the tree sheds its leaves, the leaf colour may change, as less green chlorophyll is made and other colours show through.

SUMMER   WINTER

An oak tree sheds around 250,000 leaves a year.

EVERGREEN TREES

An evergreen tree has leaves all year round and these leaves remain green. Most trees that have needles for leaves are evergreen. These leaves have been adapted to slow down the loss of water vapour, allowing them to survive in cold and dry seasons. They have a wax-like waterproof coating.

TREES HAVE LEAVES OF MANY DIFFERENT SHAPES AND SIZES

Simple

Doubly-serrate

Compound or lobed

Star-shaped

Heart-shaped or cordate

Lanceolate

Linear

Deltoid

100 SPECIES OF MOSS GROW IN THE ANTARCTIC

Few plants are able to grow in very dry or cold places, or where there isn't much sunlight.

Out of the **16,236 species of moss** in the world, only **100** grow in the Antarctic. **Six different species** of moss grow on the islands of East Antarctica. The mosses that survive here have an unusual food source. In addition to the sunlight they get from photosynthesis, they get extra nutrients from penguin poo left behind **thousands of years ago**.

1 year
2 years
3 years

The mosses on the islands of East Antarctica grow just **three millimetres** a year.

BIOMES

The Earth is often divided up into different biomes. These are places that have specific temperatures and landscapes that allow certain plants to grow there.

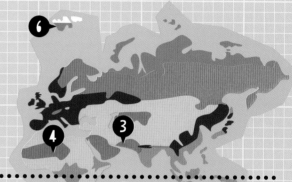

Equator

BIOMES:
- **Tundra:** treeless, cold climate
- **Taiga:** forested areas with wet summers and long cold winters
- **Grasslands:** vast grassy terrain with hot summers and cold winters
- **Desert:** dry and hot with little plant growth
- **Tropical rainforest:** hot and wet densely forested regions
- **Temperate rainforest:** cool and wet forested regions
- **Polar:** very cold with permanent presence of ice and snow

ANTARCTICA ❶

Coldest place on Earth
Average temperature: -57°C
Coldest recorded temperature: -89.2°C
The majority of the Antarctic continent is covered by permanent ice and snow leaving less than **1% of land** suitable for plants to grow. Due to the cold, harsh conditions on Antarctica, no trees are able to grow there, but some mosses have adapted to the conditions.

ATACAMA DESERT, CHILE 2
Driest place on Earth
Average temperature: 22°C
A cactus can grow in hot, dry places like deserts. Its roots are near the top of the ground so that it can take in water quickly when it rains. It stores water in its stem.

Only **three cacti** are native to this region. As it rains very little here, these cacti get the majority of their water from the ocean fog that blows over the desert.

DASHT-E LUT, IRAN 3
Hottest place on Earth
Highest recorded temperature: 70°C
No plants or creatures are recorded as living here.

SAHARA DESERT, AFRICA 4
Average temperature: 30°C
Some plants in the Sahara Desert have extensive root systems that can go deep into the ground to get water. The roots of the welwitschia mirabilis go as deep as **50 metres**.

AMAZON RAINFOREST, BRAZIL 5
Average temperature: 27°C
The Amazon rainforest has a tropical climate, providing a constant supply of water and sunlight for broad-leafed plants.

40,000 different plant species can be found here. This is the largest variety of plant species to be found in one area.

SVALBARD, NORWAY 6
Average temperature: 4°C
Only **165 species of plant** have been found to survive the tundra of Svalbard.

The Arctic buttercup lives here and is able to survive by living in groups close to the ground, sheltering them from the strong cold winds.

UNDERWATER
Seagrasses, found near the coastal waters of most continents, are the only plants that can produce flowers underwater. They are pollinated by the waves, which carry their pollen.

80-85 COCOA BEANS IN AN AVERAGE CHOCOLATE BAR

Plants provide a main source of food for all living creatures. Humans eat fruit and vegetables raw or cooked and also as an ingredient in other foods, such as chocolate or bread.

THE WORLD'S LARGEST CUCUMBER MEASURED 1.1 METRES.

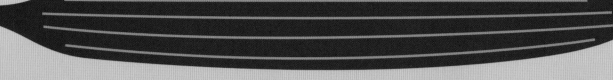

Fruit grows from the flower of a plant, but vegetables come from different parts of different plants.

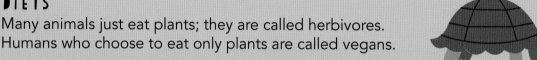

ROOTS: CARROTS

STEM: ASPARAGUS

LEAVES: CABBAGES

FLOWER: BROCCOLI

DIETS

Many animals just eat plants; they are called herbivores. Humans who choose to eat only plants are called vegans.

It's important to have a balanced diet. This means eating a variety of foods, ensuring that you receive the right nutrients that your body needs to stay healthy. Some nutrients are easily found in meat and dairy products, but if you are a vegan it's important that you eat the right foods to supplement this.

WHAT YOUR BODY NEEDS:

Examples of food it can be found in:

PROTEIN
Potatoes
Beans and pulses

CALCIUM
Broccoli
Almonds
Kale
Dried apricots

IRON
Swiss chard
Chickpeas
Lentils
Kidney beans

VITAMINS
Carrots
Oranges
Bananas
Spinach

BEANS AND PULSES

Beans and pulses are edible seeds from plants. They are often contained within protective pods and include lentils, black beans, chickpeas, broad beans and kidney beans.
Lentils have been found in the tombs of ancient Egyptians, dating back to **2400 BCE**.

CACAO TREE

COCOA BEANS COME FROM COCOA PODS WHICH COME FROM THE CACAO TREE.

Over **3,500,000 tonnes of cocoa beans** are produced annually to be transformed into products that contain cocoa.
80–85 cocoa beans go into an average chocolate bar.

The cacao tree is an evergreen, found in over **50 tropical countries**. It grows best when **15 degrees** north or south of the equator.

Cocoa beans are farmed in the following countries:
Ecuador
Brazil
Ivory Coast
Ghana
Nigeria
Cameroon
Indonesia
Kenya
Tanzania

FROM CACAO TREE TO CHOCOLATE BAR

It takes **two to three years** after the cacao tree has been planted before it produces cocoa pods, its fruit.

Every year, cacao trees grow thousands of flowers. Only around **5%** of the flowers will produce a pod.

It takes around **five months** for each pod to ripen. Once they have been cut down, the beans are then removed from their pods. There are between **30–40 beans** inside a pod.

Next, the beans are dried, often in the sun. People rake them to help the moisture escape. This takes about **one week**.

The beans are fermented to bring out the flavour and prevent them from sprouting. This is done by wrapping heaps of beans in leaf parcels or placing layers of beans in wooden crates.

The chocolate liquor is blended with some cocoa butter and other ingredients, such as sugar and milk. It is mixed for hours and then poured into chocolate bar molds.

The dried beans are taken to a processing plant where they are cleaned and roasted.

The beans pass through rollers. This leaves chocolate liquor, cocoa powder and cocoa butter.

The individual bars are wrapped and delivered across the world for people to eat.

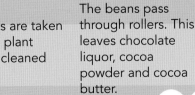
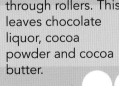

25

IT TAKES 14 TREES TO MAKE ONE TONNE OF MAGAZINE PAPER

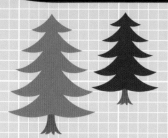

Plants not only provide you with food but feature in items all around you, such as clothes and furniture.

Paper and card are used as packaging for almost everything. Around **42%** of logging that takes place each year is for the production of paper.

= one tonne

It takes **14 trees** to make **one tonne** of magazine paper. An average magazine weighs around **350 grams**. There are **1,000,000 grams** in **one tonne**. We can divide this weight into the weight measurement of an average magazine to work out how many magazines can be produced by one tonne of paper.

The weight of one magazine divided into one tonne = **2,857 magazines**.
It takes **14 trees** to make **2,857 magazines**.
It takes one tree to make **204 magazines**. . . . . = 204

COTTON

The majority of clothes worn in the world are made from cotton.

Cotton grows as a soft fluffy ball that protects the seeds on cotton plants. Around **25 million tonnes of cotton** are grown each year.

Cotton was first used for clothing over **7,000 years ago**, in the Indus Valley, which is now part of India and Pakistan.

Plants are also used for dyeing clothes. This started over **5,000 years ago.** Plants that have been used for dye include:

Kamala tree = red   **Pomegranate peel** = yellow

Indigo fera plant = blue

MEDICINES

For hundreds of years plants have been used as medicines. Today, many extracts from plants are still used within medicines. **25%** of all medicines have been developed from tropical rainforest plants.

FOSSIL FUELS

Coal, gas and oil are known as fossil fuels. They are formed from plants and small animals that died and rotted over **millions of years**, covered by many layers of dirt deep within the ground. We use coal, gas and oil as fuel. We burn these to keep us warm and to power cars and electricity. Oil is also used to make plastics.

OCEAN 300-400,000,000 YEARS AGO

Plants and animals died and were buried under layers of sand.

OCEAN 50-100,000,000 YEARS AGO

Sand and silt

Plant and animal remains

Over millions of years these remains were buried deeper, with heat and pressure turning them into fossil fuels, such as oil and gas.

TODAY

Sand and silt rock

Oil and gas

We drill down through layers of sand and rock to reach the fossil fuels.

PLANT	USED FOR
Foxglove	Heart medication
Eucalyptus tree	Cough medicine
Quinine tree	Malaria prevention
Opium poppy	Pain reliever
Curare tree	Muscle relaxant

THE QUEEN OF THE NIGHT BLOOMS FOR ONE NIGHT EVERY YEAR

Amongst the huge number of plant life there exist some unusual plants that can amaze and disgust.

CORPSE FLOWERS

DISGUSTING PLANTS

The titan arum, found in Indonesia, is one of the world's smelliest plants. It produces flowers about every six years and when this happens, it smells like rotten meat. Because of this, it is also known as the 'corpse flower'. The flowering structure can reach up to **three metres** in height. It is surrounded by a single leaf which can grow to **six metres** tall and **five metres** wide.

RAFFLESIA ARNOLDII

1 metre

1.70 metres is the height of an average adult human being.

TITAN ARUM

Height in metres

3

3.5

2

2.5

2

1.5

1

0

The rafflesia arnoldii, from Indonesia, is also sometimes called a 'corpse flower' as it too smells of rotting meat. It has the largest flower of any plant in the world. Its flower has a diameter of around **one metre**. The rafflesia lives as a parasite on other plants.

PARASITIC PLANTS

Plants that attach themselves to other plants, and suck out nutrients from them, are known as parasitic plants. These plants manage to insert roots into their host plant.

Mistletoe is a parasitic plant. Its seeds land on their host plant in bird poo. They can grow large and bushy, to the point where it can be hard to spot the host plant's leaves amongst those of the mistletoe.

MISTLETOE ON AN APPLE TREE

GIANT WATER LILY

LARGE LEAVES

The giant water lily has a large circular leaf, also known as a lily pad, that can grow to over **2.5 metres** in diameter. The leaf can support **45 kilograms** of weight, provided it is evenly distributed over the leaf's surface.

FOR ONE NIGHT ONLY

The night-blooming cereus, also known as the 'queen of the night', is the name of a group of cacti that flower at night. Some of these only flower once a year. They grow in the deserts of Texas, the USA and north Mexico. The flowers are trumpet-shaped, up to **10 centimetres** wide and **20 centimetres** long.

NIGHT-BLOOMING CEREUS

FURTHER INFORMATION

BOOKS

Project Science: Plants by Sally Hewitt (Franklin Watts, 2012)

Science F.A.Q.: Do Plants Really Eat Insects? by Thomas Canavan (Franklin Watts, 2016)

Living Processes: Plant Variation and Classification by Dr Carol Ballard (Wayland, 2015)

The World in Infographics: The Natural World by Jon Richards and Ed Simkins (Wayland, 2015)

WEBSITES

Games and information on how to grow plants and information on the environmental issues surrounding tropical rainforests:

www.sciencekids.co.nz/plants.html

Activity with instructions on how to grow your own miniature garden:

kids.nationalgeographic.com/kids/activities/crafts/miniature-garden/

Information on the importance of trees with links to games:

www.ecokids.ca/pub/eco_info/topics/climate/tree_planting/why_plant_trees.cfm

Note to parents and teachers:

Every effort has been made by the publisher to ensure that these websites contain no inappropriate or offensive material. However, because of the nature of the Internet, it is impossible to guarantee that the content of these sites will not be altered. We strongly advise that Internet access is supervised by a responsible adult.

LARGE NUMBERS

1,000,000,000,000,000,000,000,000,000,000,000 = ONE DECILLION

1,000,000,000,000,000,000,000,000,000,000 = ONE NONILLION

1,000,000,000,000,000,000,000,000,000 = ONE OCTILLION

1,000,000,000,000,000,000,000,000 = ONE SEPTILLION

1,000,000,000,000,000,000,000 = ONE SEXTILLION

1,000,000,000,000,000,000 = ONE QUINTILLION

1,000,000,000,000,000 = ONE QUADRILLION

1,000,000,000,000 = ONE TRILLION

1,000,000,000 = ONE BILLION

1,000,000 = ONE MILLION

1000 = ONE THOUSAND

100 = ONE HUNDRED

10 = TEN

1 = ONE

GLOSSARY

algae	a simple form of plant often found in water. Some seaweeds are algae
allergic reaction	when your body reacts to a particular substance, causing iritation, such as itchy eyes or a rash
biomes	large areas on Earth that are defined by their plant life and climate
botany	the scientific study of plants
carbon dioxide	a gas that humans breathe out and plants absorb
carnivorous	the description of an organism that eats animals
chlorophyll	a green pigment found in plants that helps them absorb light and produce their food
conifers	trees and shrubs that have cones, and are mostly evergreen
deciduous	trees that shed their leaves during a season of the year
dehydration	when something is dry, after water loss
endangered	at risk of extinction
estimate	an approximate calculation
evergreen	a plant that has leaves which remain green all year round
evolved	when something has developed over a long period of time
extinct	having no living members; a species that has died out
fossil fuel	fuel made up of the remains of organisms that have been compressed underground
frond	a large leaf, like those on a fern, that splits into different sections
germination	the process whereby something begins to grow and develop, such as a seedling sprouting out from a seed
grafting	attaching one part of a plant to another plant to grow together
habitat	the environment or home of a creature or plant
herbivore	the description of an organism that only eats plants
invasive species	organisms that invade and modify an environment of which they are not naturally a part
liverwort	small green non-flowering plant, similar to moss but with a more distinctive leaf structure
moss	green, dense, non-flowering plant that grows in damp areas
nectar	a sugary substance produced by plants and made into honey by bees
nutrients	a substance that is beneficial to growth and well-being
organism	a living thing
oxygen	a gas that plants produce and humans breathe in to live
parasite	an organism that lives off another organism
photosynthesis	the process by which plants create their own food and produce oxygen
pollen	dust-like grains on a flower that are required to be carried to another plant for fertilisation
pollination	the process whereby pollen is transferred from one plant to another
rhizome	an underground root-like structure that bears shoots
sap	a fluid that circulates around a plant, carrying nutrients and water
species	living things that contain shared characteristics, e.g. human beings
spores	the reproductive cells of ferns and mosses
stamen	the fertilising organ of a plant
toxic	a poisonous substance

INDEX